Secrets of Adobe Bridge

Making the Most of Adobe Creative Suite 2

Terry White

Adobe

Secrets of Adobe Bridge: Making the Most of Adobe Creative Suite 2
Terry White

This Adobe Press book is published by Peachpit

For information on Adobe Press books, contact:
Peachpit
1249 Eighth Street
Berkeley, CA 94710
510/524-2178
800/283-9444
510/524-2221 (fax)

To report errors, please send a note to errata@peachpit.com
Peachpit is a division of Pearson Education

For the latest on Adobe Press books, go to
www.adobepress.com

Editor: Nancy Davis
Production Editor: Becky Winter
Compositor: Diana Van Winkle
Proofreader: Amy Standen
Indexer: FireCrystal Communications
Interior design: Diana Van Winkle
Cover design: Charlene Charles-Will

ISBN 0-321-39227-2

9 8 7 6 5 4 3 2 1

Printed and bound in the United States of America

*For my lovely wife Carla for allowing me the opportunity
to pursue my dreams, and for my two beautiful daughters
Ayoola and Sala, for providing me with constant
inspiration and motivation.*

Acknowledgments

Writing this book would not have been possible without the constant support of my family, friends, and colleagues. While there aren't enough pages to thank and acknowledge everyone, I would like to acknowledge my wife Carla who has constantly supported my efforts; my two daughters Ayoola and Sala, both visions of beauty and motivation; my sister Pam who is always there for me to bounce ideas and problems off of; and, of course, my mom and dad for bringing me into this world and raising me right.

I would like to thank all of my friends, team members, managers, and colleagues at Adobe, including Sue Scheen, Colin Fleming, Lynn Grillo, Robert McDaniels, Adam Pratt, Mike Richman, Colin Smith, Dean Velez, Steve Whatley, Jonathan Bowman, Noha Edell, John Nack, Ashwini Jambotkar, Gary Cosmini, Lisa Forrester, Tim Cole, Julieanne Kost, Peggy Snyder, Russell Preston Brown, Dave Helmly, Lisa Avalos, Donna Zontos, the entire Americas Sales Team, and the Digital Imaging Product Team.

I must give special thanks to one of my best buddies, Scott Kelby, who encouraged me to get started writing books. I owe much of my publishing success to him and his tireless efforts to be the best!

I would also like to thank all my friends in the Mac community for their continued support and help over the years, especially Steve Wozniak, Sandy Kaye, Mary and Joseph Grey, Mia Sasser, Mike Arlow, Carmela Z. Robertson, Chita Hunter, Shirley Kussner, Lori Autrey, Phyllis Evans, David Syme, Kwesi Ohene Aquil, Piankhi Blount, and Leonard Mazerov.

I also want to thank my wonderful editor Nancy Davis for doing such an awesome job on this book and being so easy to work with.

— TERRY WHITE

Contents

2 Organizing Files 15

3 Managing Files in the Bridge 31

Introduction

In the Adobe Creative Suite 2, the Adobe Bridge takes the functionality that we knew and loved in the Photoshop File Browser and makes it a stand-alone application. If you think about the way you used the File Browser in Photoshop—to view folders of images without having to open the individual files, rename files, and launch them—the Bridge does that and more for all your creative applications. And now, this functionality is no longer tied to just Photoshop. Because the Bridge is a stand-alone application, you can launch it and organize your files independently of Photoshop or any other application. You can use the Bridge to browse all kinds of file types, such as InDesign and Illustrator documents. You can even browse and preview multiple-page PDFs and QuickTime movies.

I hate to use a drug reference, but the Adobe Bridge is like the File Browser on steroids. Steroids get such a bad rap, but the comparison is accurate. The more I use the Bridge, the more I want to use the Bridge. It's addictive—hmmm, I don't like where this is going, so let's move on.

In this book I plan to show you everything I can about the Bridge, and to also give you ideas on how you can use the Bridge to enhance your workflow and to (pardon the pun) bridge the gap between all your Adobe CS2 applications.

There are two ways to get the Bridge: you can get it by buying any one of the Adobe CS2 stand-alone applications. You can also get the Bridge as a part of the Adobe Creative Suite 2. The basic functionality is the same between the two versions. However, if you are a Creative Suite 2 owner you will have three added capabilities: you'll be able to synchronize your

continues on next page

color management settings across all your Creative Suite 2 applications. You'll also be able to use Bridge scripts that apply to each of the Creative Suite 2 applications, such as creating a contact sheet in InDesign CS2 or doing a Live Trace of a selected image in Illustrator CS2. And lastly, the Bridge that comes with the Creative Suite also includes the Bridge Center, which you can think of as your Creative Pro desktop. It will keep track of things like the last files and folders you accessed, saved search collections, and it even features a built-in RSS newsreader. So with all the excitement I've just caused, I won't hold you back anymore. Let's get started learning the Secrets of the Bridge.

Navigating the Interface

If you've used the File Browser in previous versions of Photoshop, then you're going to feel right at home in the Bridge. By default the Bridge is a one window application divided into four panes. The upper-left pane contains your Favorites and Folders. The pane on the middle left is your Preview palette, and this is the area that will show you the contents of a file that you select. The pane on the lower left contains your Metadata and Keywords palettes. The biggest window to the right is the thumbnail view.

Navigating to a Folder of Images

In order to get started with the Bridge, the first thing you'll need to do is navigate to a folder with at least a few images in it. Luckily, Adobe makes this pretty easy by putting some default Favorites in the folder for you. On the Mac, you'll be able to access your Desktop, Documents, and Pictures folders, and on Windows, you'll be able to access your Desktop, My Documents, and My Pictures folders. So if you have already been putting your pictures in any of these places you can simply click on the folder to show you the contents of it, including any subfolders. However, if the images or documents that you want to browse are located in another folder or perhaps on another drive, you can click on the Folders tab. From there you can navigate to any drive, disc, or other volume you have access to on your computer.

There are two ways to use the Folders tab. The first way is to simply click or double-click on a drive or a folder, and you will start to see the contents of that drive or folder in the main window. You can then continue navigating your way down the folder tree by double-clicking the enclosed folders. This way is going to take the longest because for each folder you view, the Bridge will start to build the icons for each document. If you want to go faster, don't click on the folder itself. Instead click on the little arrow pointing to the folder to twirl it down (PC: Click the little plus sign in front of the folder). This allows you to see the enclosed folders without building the icon previews for every single folder in the tree. Once you get down to the folder you want you can then click on it to see its contents.

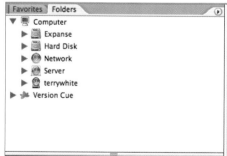

Changing the Size of your Thumbnails

The most common way that people will look at their images in the Bridge is in an icon view. This will feel very natural to photographers and layout artists because it's reminiscent of a light box and looking at slides or other artwork. However, one thumbnail size does not fit all. In the old Photoshop File Browser you were limited to only a few default sizes, such as small, medium, and large. Luckily, with the new Bridge, you can achieve many more thumbnail sizes by dragging the slider along the bottom of the Bridge window. At the smallest size you can probably barely make out the image. However, this small thumbnail allows you see many more documents at once and is useful if you're looking for something by name instead of by appearance. Remember, the Bridge isn't just for images. Also keep in mind that any image you click on will display larger in the Preview palette no matter how small the thumbnail is.

Tip: When you're browsing a folder of files you can just start typing the name of the file that you want to get to and Bridge will take you to it.

To increase the size of the thumbnails, simply drag the slider to the right until the thumbnails are as large as you like.

Showing and Hiding the Folders, Preview, and Metadata Palettes

Now that you've gotten a good handle on sizing your icons, you're probably still going to want to maximize your thumbnail viewing area from time to time. The Folders, Preview, and Metadata palettes all exist in a panel that can be exposed or hidden with a single click. In the lower-left corner of the Bridge is a set of arrows pointing left and right. This is actually a button that allows you to Show or Hide the panel on the left. One click hides it, another click brings it back. When the panel is hidden, you have much more room to see your thumbnails. You'll still be able to use most of the Bridge functions with the panel hidden, including double-clicking on files to launch them and using the navigation buttons at the top of the window.

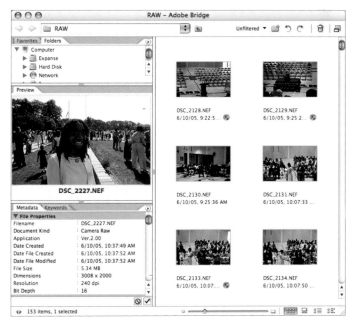

With palettes visible

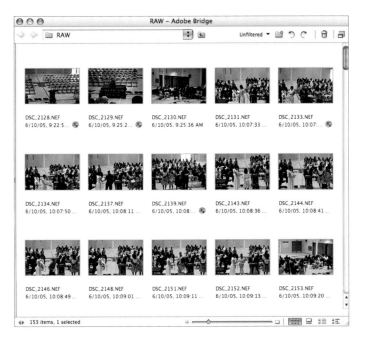

With palettes hidden

Rearranging Tabs

As I stated earlier, the Bridge is basically a one window application. Granted, you can have multiple windows open, but for the most part you can get everything done in one window. This is really a departure from most traditional Adobe applications that have floating palettes. The Bridge does have palettes on the left panel, they just don't float. However, just because they don't float doesn't mean that you can't rearrange them. By default the Bridge displays your Favorites and Folders palettes at the top, your Preview palette in the middle, and your Metadata and Keywords palettes at the bottom. You can rearrange these tabs any way you want simply by clicking and dragging on the tab and dropping it in one of the existing areas. You can even combine the tabs into fewer areas. For example, if you drag the Preview palette down to the Metadata and Keyword area you will now only have two panes along the left, instead of three. Before panic sets in—and I just went through this myself as I was testing this just now—if you want to get back to have three or more panes on the left, simply drag a tab to the horizontal line that separates the panes and it will insert it as a new area. You can also drag a tab all the way to the top or bottom of the panel area to insert it at the top or bottom.

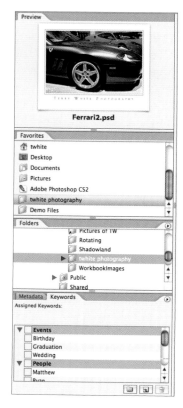

Expanding the Preview Palette

The tab that you're likely to spend a lot of time in is the Preview palette. After all, the Preview palette is where you look when you click on an image to see it larger. The problem is that the Preview palette may not be much larger than the thumbnails themselves. Well there is some good news. You can resize the Preview palette to be as large as you like. There are a couple of ways to do this. The first way—and this is one that you may have already figured out—is to grab the dividing bars and pull them away from the Preview palette to make the Preview palette larger. You'll notice there are little handles on the bars themselves that look like three short lines. Although these handles are there as a visual reminder that the bars can be pulled, you can actually pull anywhere along the bar to resize them. That's why this book is called *Secrets of the Bridge*.

Another way to get your Preview palette even larger is to collapse the palettes that you're not using. For example, if you not using the Metadata and Keywords palettes you can collapse them to make your Preview palette larger. To collapse a tab, simply double-click on the tab's name. As you have undoubtedly guessed, double-clicking the name of the tab will expand it. So if you wanted the maximum Preview palette, you could collapse Metadata/Keywords and Favorites/Folders.

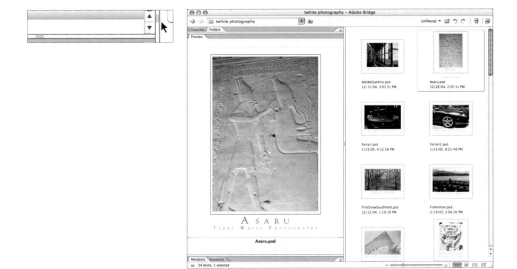

Switching Viewing Modes

Earlier I said, "One thumbnail size does not fit all." The same applies to the thumbnail view in general. In the default thumbnail view you can see the thumbnail, rating, color label, filename, and modification date/time. The main window will show you as many thumbnails as it can across and down based on the thumbnail size you've chosen with the slider.

When thumbnails aren't enough, there are other views to use.

You can switch view modes by clicking on the icon for the mode you want to use in the lower-right corner of the Bridge window.

Filmstrip View

What if you want to see your thumbnails and a nice large preview at the same time? There's a view for that. It's called Filmstrip view. Filmstrip view allows you to see nice small thumbnails and a larger preview above the thumbnails without having to resize your Preview palette on the left. You can then navigate your images using the left and right onscreen buttons, or better yet, the left and right arrow keys on your keyboard. You can also switch to a vertical Filmstrip view by clicking the little button to the right of the onscreen navigation arrows. Having this flexibility allows you to take greater advantage of large displays, such as the Apple Cinema Display.

Details View

When filenames and dates are not enough you can switch to the Details view by clicking the third button to the right of the thumbnail size slider (circled, below). In the Details view you get to see more of the metadata contained in the file, such as the author of the file. You also get to see the date created and date modified, file size, pixel dimensions, color space, and document type. The thumbnails are still at a decent size and you still have the flexibility to use the slider to resize them.

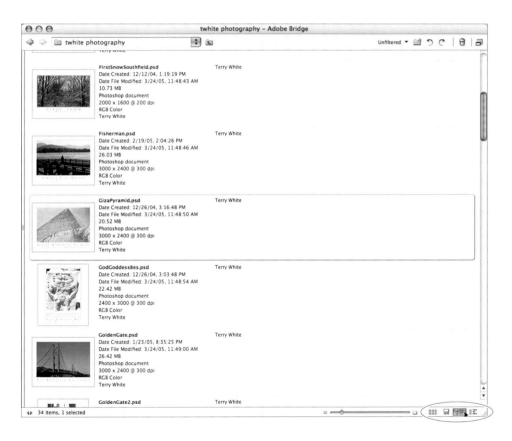

Versions and Alternates View

The last view for the main window is the Versions and Alternates view. This view is really only used when you are using Version Cue, which is a part of the Adobe Creative Suite 2. The Bridge can browse your Version Cue file managed projects and show you the current and previous versions of a file, including the current version comments. It's very handy to be able to see previous versions of a file at a glance, as this allows you to know what possibilities you have in reverting back to a previous version. It also shows you the date and time of each version so you'll immediately know how fast or slowly a project is progressing.

Alternates is a new feature to Creative Suite 2. Now not only can a file have previous versions, but it can also have Alternate versions of a file. For example, let's say you took two shots of a car—a shot that looks at the car head on and a shot that looks at the car from the side. If you modified the head-on shot of the car, you could save each modification as a new version. By doing this, you would always be able to revert back to a previous version by promoting it to be the current version. Version Cue keeps track of all versions until you decide to delete them. However, with Alternates you could make the side shot the Alternate view of the car. Adobe InDesign CS2 supports placing files managed in Version Cue CS2 and therefore also supports switching to Alternates view. This way you could place one file on your InDesign page and then choose the Alternates view without having to replace the image each time. By clicking the Alternates view button you can see if the files in your Version Cue folder have any alternates. If that's not enough to make your head spin, keep in mind that each alternate can have multiple versions, too.

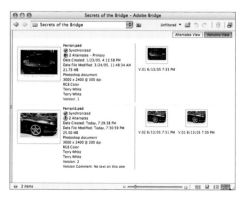

Compact Mode and Ultra-Compact Mode

It's great that the Bridge is a separate application. However, because it's a separate application, you can sometimes feel like it's in the way. After all, you probably want to keep the size of your Bridge window fairly large so that you can see more thumbnails and bigger previews, right? Of course, this means that it would be a large window blocking any other window that you're working in. The Bridge supports three operating modes. *Full Mode* is what you're used to, and it's what we've been working in up to this point. Full Mode shows you every panel and every button that's available in the Bridge.

Compact Mode shrinks the window to a much smaller size, and by default, floats it above all your other application windows. This is cool because you can use the Bridge as a drag-and-drop image palette for any application that supports dragging and dropping images, such as Adobe InDesign CS2. No matter which application you switch to, the Bridge window will stay on top. You can turn off this behavior in the Bridge menu in the upper-right corner

of the Bridge while you're in Compact Mode. You can get back to Full Mode by clicking the Switch to Full Mode button in the upper-right corner, to the left of the Bridge menu.

There is one more mode that's even more compact than Compact Mode. It's called *Ultra-Compact Mode*. While you're in Compact Mode you have the option of going to Full Mode or Ultra-Compact Mode. You can switch to Ultra-Compact Mode using the button just to the left of the Switch to Full Mode button in the upper-right corner of the Bridge window. While you're in Ultra-Compact Mode, there isn't a whole lot you can do. This mode is designed to make the window as small as possible because you're trying to see something behind it. I must admit, as much of a fan of the Bridge as I am, I rarely use Ultra-Compact Mode. It's just as easy to minimize the Bridge application or simply switch to the application that I'm trying to see. When you're in Compact Mode or Ultra-Compact Mode, the button in the top-right corner becomes a toggle between these two modes. Switch to Full Mode is always available.

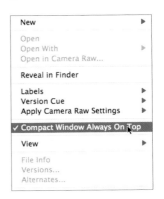

continues on next page

Compact Mode is the only mode that supports the "Always On Top feature." This keeps the Bridge window on top of any other window from any other application. This is great when you want to drag and drop from the Bridge to other applications as the Bridge window won't get accidentally buried behind other windows.

Setting the Background Display

By default, the background display behind your thumbnails is a neutral gray color. Some prefer to have it be white or black or maybe even a darker shade of gray. Rather than try to pick the shade that everyone was going to want, Adobe did the next best thing: they gave us a slider that allows us to pick the background shade of our choice. To change the background display, follow these simple steps:

Step 1: Choose Preferences from the Bridge menu (PC: Choose Preferences from the Edit menu).

Step 2: Drag the Background slider towards Black to make the background darker and towards White to make it lighter.

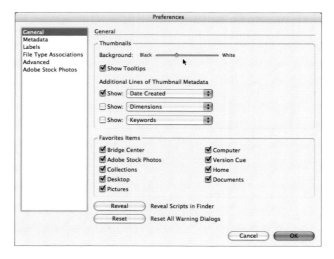

Step 3: Click OK and verify that you like the new setting better. If not, simply return to the Preferences and try a different setting with the Background slider.

Opening Multiple Bridge Windows

Although the Bridge operates as a one-window application, you can have more than one Bridge window open at once. This is great if you're trying to compare the contents of two windows. Or maybe you want to view the contents of one of your folders and the Bridge Center (the launch pad portion of the Bridge that comes with the Creative Suite) at the same time. It's very easy to get a new Bridge window. Simply choose New Window from the File menu and you can set the view of your new window to any folder or any mode that you want. Also, by having more than one Bridge window open at a time, you can easily drag files from one window to the next. Think of it as having two Finder windows (PC: Folders) open at the same time. You do it all the time in the operating system. Now you can do it in the Bridge, too.

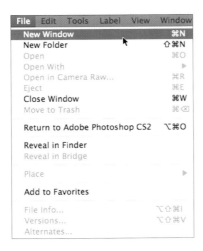

Working with Workspaces

Workspaces allow you to save your window configurations in the Bridge by name so that you can quickly recall them as needed. Workspaces have become a standard feature across the Adobe Creative Suite product line. They really come in handy for quickly switching palettes around. Although the Bridge doesn't really have any floating palettes, you can still use the Workspace feature to control the left panel and palette configurations inside it.

Step 1: Arrange the Bridge the way you like it. Change the side panel sizes and change the thumbnail sizes.

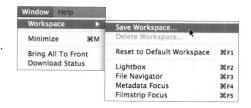

Step 2: Choose Save Workspace from the Window > Workspace menu.

Step 3: In the Save Workspace dialog box, give the workspace a name and decide if you want to give it a keyboard shortcut as well as remember the location of the window.

Step 4: Click Save.

Now whenever you want to switch to this workspace you can either choose it from the Window > Workspace menu or you can use the keyboard shortcut that you assigned to it. Even if you don't create your own workspace, Adobe gives you some pretty useful ones by default, such as Lightbox, File Navigator, Metadata Focus, and Filmstrip Focus. You can even choose one of these and modify what it does in the Bridge and then save it as a new workspace.

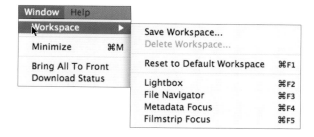

2 Organizing Files

One of the main functions of the Adobe Bridge is organizing your files. There are many different approaches to file organization. You could organize your files by project, file type, color space, etc. Whichever method you decide on, the Bridge can handle it. Think of the Bridge as a window into your computer's file system. No files actually get stored in the Bridge. Instead, the Bridge looks into the files and folders on your computer's hard drive. So if you delete or rename a file in the Bridge, you're actually renaming the file just as if you had gone to the Finder or the Windows Explorer to do it.

Sorting Files

Looking at files in the Bridge only
brings up the natural desire to see the
files in a specific order. By default, the
Bridge shows your files in ascending
order by *Filename*. And for the most
part you'll probably keep it that way.
However, it's my job as author to
point out that you have many more
options for sorting.

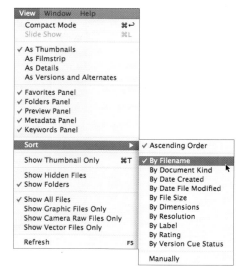

You can also sort by *Document Kind*,
which will group all the like documents together such as PDFs, TIFFs,
PSDs, etc. You can sort by *Date Created*
or *Date File Modified*, which will help
you locate files by which ones are
oldest or newest. You can even sort
by *File Size*, *Dimensions*, and *Resolution*, which will help you determine which
files are suitable for print and which ones should probably be left for video
and the Web. You can also sort by *Label* and *Rating*, as well as *Version Cue
Status*. To sort by any of these options, simply choose Sort from the View
menu and you can select which way you want to sort the window you're
currently viewing.

Setting Manual Sort Order

Having your documents in a nice ascending order by filename is great.
However, there will be times that you will want to "arrange" your images
in a custom order. Perhaps you want
to build a PDF Presentation or you
want to show the best images at the
top and have your just okay images
at the bottom. If you had a physical
light table, you'd be able to simply
drag the images or documents around
in the order you wanted. The Bridge
works that way too. Even if you pick
a specific sort order, you can simply

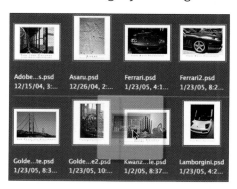

move the images around by dragging them and the Bridge will automatically assume you want a custom sort order. So you don't have to actually go to the Sort menu and choose Manually. You simply drag the files around in the window in the order you want.

Narrowing Down What the Bridge Shows You

Thumbnail only

By default, the Bridge shows you the Filename, Date Created, and Time Created under each thumbnail. You can turn off this text display and just see the thumbnails by choosing "Show Thumbnail Only" from the View menu. The keyboard shortcut is Command-T (PC: Control-T). Pressing this keyboard command toggles the Thumbnail Only view on or off.

Invisible files

The default Bridge view shows the same files that
you would see in the Finder (PC: Windows Explorer).
However, both Mac OS X and Windows support invisible files. These files are typically used by the system
and they are not intended to be interacted with by
the user. That's why they are invisible or hidden. The
Bridge has the ability to see invisible files. I can't
think of too many reasons why you would need to do
this as a creative pro or photographer, but as a user
who likes to get under the hood of the computer, this
is one of the easiest ways to see those forbidden files.

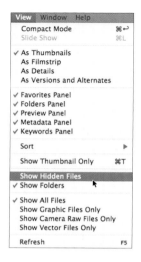

Before I tell you how to do this I must warn you
that the OS hides files for a reason. If you rename or
delete the wrong hidden file by accident you could
cause an application or your entire operating sys-
tem to stop working. If that makes you feel funny inside, then skip to the
next section. If you want to see your hidden files, simply point to a folder
that you suspect has hidden files such as the main hard drive window and
choose Show Hidden Files from the View menu to see the underworld that is
your computer. Once the excitement wears off you can simply choose Show
Hidden Files again to turn it off.

File Types

By default, the Bridge shows you all the files in a
selected folder. So if you pointed the Bridge to your
Documents folder, you would see all kinds of files,
such as Microsoft Word documents, PDFs, graphic
files, etc. If you're just looking for a picture, the Bridge
can narrow that view down for you. When you choose
the View menu you notice that it says Show All Files
near the bottom and it's checked. If you choose to
Show Graphic Files Only it will narrow the folder
down to just graphic files and folders. You can also
choose to show just the Camera Raw files or just the
Vector Files, such as Adobe Illustrator documents or
EPS files.

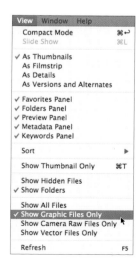

Ratings

In the old Photoshop File Browser you could mark a document as flagged or unflagged and then show just the flagged files or the unflagged files or both. The Bridge takes this functionality to a whole new level by allowing you to rate your documents with one to five stars. This means you don't have to live with just good or bad. You can now make up your own rating systems. Perhaps one star documents should never be shown in public. Two star documents may only be shown to family members. Three star documents could be shown to clients. Four star documents are documents you could probably charge for and five star documents should go in your portfolio. Of course you can make up your own rules.

You can rate a single document or multiple documents at the same time by selecting them in the Bridge window and choosing the desired number of stars from the Label menu. For your convenience, the Ratings feature also has keyboard shortcuts. You could use Command-1 to give your document a one star rating, Command-2 to give it a two star rating, etc (on the PC it would be Control-1, Control-2, etc.). If you wanted to take the rating away using an easy shortcut, you could use Command-0 (PC: Control-0).

Tip: Hitting Command-T (PC: Control-T) toggles off the file name, ratings, and labels. The screen now resembles a light table with just the images. Hitting Command-T (PC: Control-T) again toggles the information display back on.

Labels

Color labels offer a very visual way of organizing your files. In addition to star ratings, you can assign your documents one of five different color labels (Red, Yellow, Green, Blue, or Purple). Once you assign color labels to your documents you can then sort by those colors. Color labels are assigned to documents in almost the same manner as ratings. You select the documents that you want to label and choose the label color you want from the Label menu. Just like ratings you can also assign labels from the keyboard: Command-6 for Red, Command-7 for Yellow, Command-8 for Green, and Command-9 for Blue. Purple does not have a keyboard command. (PC: Use Control and numbers 6–9 for the same results.) You can also assign labels using a contextual menu. Select the images you want and Control-click on them (PC: Right-click), and from the Label menu in the contextual menu that pops up, choose the label you want.

Filtering

Now that you've added ratings and labels to the documents in your folder, you'll probably want to narrow down the view of that folder to just show your labeled files. For example, maybe you want to see your pictures that are rated with four or five stars. Or maybe you want to see all the documents that you've assigned a Blue label. You can do this quite easily. At the top of the Bridge window is a menu that reads "Unfiltered" by default. When you pull that menu down you can choose from all the various filtering options to show you just the ratings you want or the labels you want or combinations of the two. I choose to show my documents that have three or more stars with a Yellow label.

Show All Items	⌥⌘A
Show Unrated Items Only	
Show 1 or More Stars	⌥⌘1
Show 2 or More Stars	⌥⌘2
✓ Show 3 or More Stars	⌥⌘3
Show 4 or More Stars	⌥⌘4
Show 5 Stars	⌥⌘5
Show Labeled Items Only	
Show Unlabeled Items Only	
Show Red Label	⌥⌘6
✓ Show Yellow Label	⌥⌘7
Show Green Label	⌥⌘8
Show Blue Label	⌥⌘9
Show Purple Label	

Using Slideshows

The Slideshow feature in the Bridge allows you to show a folder of images full screen and advance automatically or manually. You can do it right in the Bridge without any additional software. Because you have manual sorting capabilities, you can arrange the images in the exact order you want them to appear in the slideshow. You can use this feature to show your work to your client or to see your own work full screen. More importantly, you can use the slideshow feature to rate and label your images.

Although it's pretty cool to be able to sit back and watch a slideshow of your images go by, the Slideshow feature in the Bridge also offers some interactivity. This means that while you're manually advancing your slideshow you can assign ratings and labels. There's even a secret way to open an image directly from the slideshow while it's running. Keep reading!

Starting and Stopping a Slideshow

Once you navigate to a folder of your images that you want to display as a slideshow, you'll need to know the secret command to get the slideshow going. You can find it in the View menu. However, there is a keyboard shortcut that's even easier. Just press Command-L (PC: Control-L) and your slideshow will go to the first image and make it full screen. By the way, this is the exact same command for presenting a multiple-page PDF in Acrobat or the free Adobe Reader full screen. See, if you learn it once you can use it elsewhere in the Adobe product line.

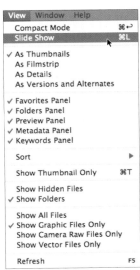

Before we go any further, you're probably going to want to know how to stop the show. As you may have guessed, you can stop the slideshow by pressing the Esc key on your keyboard. That's pretty common across presentation apps. So, no sense in breaking tradition.

Getting Help While Running a Slideshow

There are several commands that you can use while you're in a slideshow. In other applications I use Help as a last resort. I like to try to figure things out myself first. However, the way that the Help is implemented in the Bridge is unobtrusive and elegant. After starting the slideshow (Command-L; PC: Control-L), hit the H key on the keyboard. This will superimpose the slideshow Help right over your slideshow and show you the keyboard commands you'll want to know to take advantage of the slideshow. Some commands that you'll want to commit to memory are: Spacebar for playing the slideshow automatically and pausing it; left and right arrow keys to navigate the slideshow from one image to the next; and the left and right bracket keys [ ] to rotate an image without leaving the slideshow.

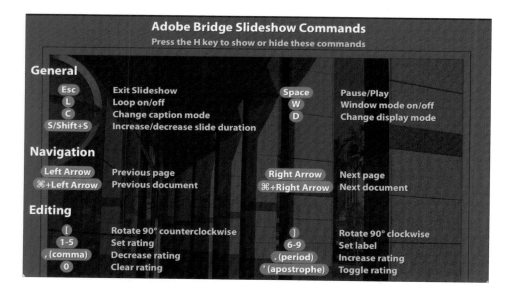

Using Manual vs. Automatic Advance

By default, the slideshow will be in manual mode, which means that the first image will be displayed and you'll have to advance to the next image when you're ready by pressing the right arrow key. You can also have the slideshow advance automatically by pressing the spacebar on your keyboard. The spacebar acts as a Play and Pause button. This will advance the slides (images/documents) by one approximately every five seconds.

Applying Ratings and Labels During the Slideshow

One of the most productive things that you can do while you're viewing a slideshow in manual mode is to apply ratings and labels. It's a natural place to do it as you will be looking at the image full screen, and the process goes quickly because you can use keyboard commands to assign the ratings and labels.

Step 1: Navigate to a folder of images.

Step 2: Enter slideshow mode by pressing Command-L (PC: Control-L).

Step 3: To assign a rating of one or more stars, press the number 1, 2, 3, 4, or 5 on your keyboard. As you have guessed at this point, each number you hit will rate the image with that many stars.

Step 4: You can assign a color label to the image by pressing 6 for Red, 7 for Yellow, 8 for Green, 9 for Blue.

Step 5: You can move to the next image by pressing the right arrow key or you can end the slideshow by pressing the Esc key.

Note: The minute you assign a rating or label you'll notice that the caption stays there from that point on. If you want to just look at your images without the caption on, you can cycle through the caption modes by pressing the letter C until the caption turns off.

Opening Files and Window Mode

OK, here's an undocumented Bridge secret, shhhhh! While you're in a slideshow you can press the letter O key to open the image/document currently on the screen in the appropriate application. For example, .psd files will open in Photoshop and .ai files will open in Illustrator, etc. I was excited to find this out. However, after I finished working on the image in Photoshop, I returned to the Bridge to find the slideshow still running. Great, however it wasn't full screen anymore. It was in "Window mode." At the time I didn't know what the mode was called, so I didn't know what to look for to switch it back to full screen. I'll save you that bit of frustration. You can toggle between full screen and Window mode by pressing the letter W on the keyboard.

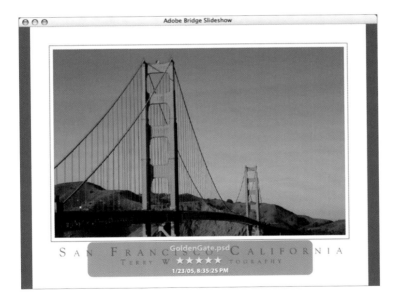

Setting Favorites

The Favorites palette is one of my favorite features of the Bridge. It allows me to put the folders, documents, and applications that I use all the time in one easy to access location. It's a great organizational tool. Favorites can contain just about anything. There are a few ways to add things to the Favorites, and we'll cover them in a moment. However, you can also control what the Bridge puts in Favorites by default by going to Preferences from the Bridge menu (PC: Edit menu) and checking or unchecking the items you want there or don't want there. For example, some companies may have their own system for buying stock photography and don't want users buying them ad hoc from the Bridge. So you could turn off the Adobe Stock Photos service and it would no longer appear in the Favorites palette.

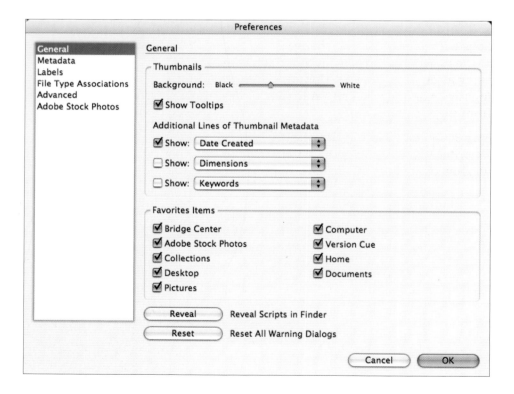

Adding Favorite Folders

Although you can add documents and applications to the Favorites palette, you'll most
likely want to add folders that you use to
store your images or projects. It's great that
the Bridge automatically adds your Pictures
folder and your Documents folder to the
Favorites, but chances are you probably have
a few folders of your own that contain the
documents you'll want to view and manage.
There are a few ways to add folders to the
Favorites:

Step 1: Navigate to the folder that you want
to add to the Favorites.

Step 2: If you're already in the folder looking
at the images, you can add it to the Favorites
using a contextual menu—Control-click (PC:
Right-click)—or by choosing Add to Favorites
from the File menu.

Step 3: You can also add a folder to the
Favorites simply by dragging it from the main
window to the Favorites palette.

Removing Favorites

As soon as the project is complete, you may want to remove the folder from the Favorites palette. To remove an item from the Favorites palette, you can Control-click on it (PC: Right-click) to get a contextual menu that offers to "Remove from Favorites." This, of course, does not remove the folder from the computer; it just removes it from the Favorites palette. You can also choose Remove from Favorites from the File menu to remove files from the Favorites palette.

3 Managing Files in the Bridge

Now that we've explored getting around in the Bridge, it's time to get some work done. The Bridge is more than just a look-and-see application. It allows you to do several functions without having to open the documents up one-by-one and since it's a stand-alone application, it can work with a variety of file types. You can do the kind of things that you do day in and day out with ease. Let's say you photograph an event. After you get back to your computer, you'll first want to download and look at your images. Well, we pretty much covered the ways to look at your images in the previous chapters. But, after looking at your images you may want to rename them. Digital cameras don't give you warm and fuzzy filenames. DSC_2117.NEF and DSC_2118.NEF don't really tell

you a lot about the image. However, Hawaii-01.jpg, Hawaii-02.jpg sounds a lot better. You may also need to rotate your images if your camera doesn't do it automatically. If you want to make your images searchable, then you'll surely want to assign meta-data and keywords. You can do all of this—and more—in the Adobe Bridge.

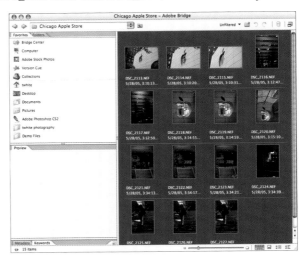

Selecting and Deselecting Files

Before you can do any of the functions we're about to cover in this chapter, you first need to get a handle on selecting and deselecting files and folders. By now you've probably discovered that you can simply click on a document in the main Bridge window to select it. Holding down the Shift key while clicking will continue to add documents to your selection. However, the Shift key selects *all* the documents in between. You can make non-contiguous selections by holding down the Command key (PC: Control key) instead of the Shift key. If you want to select everything in the folder, you can choose Select All from the Edit menu or press Command-A (PC: Control-A).

Edit	Tools	Label	View	Window	H
Undo					⌘Z
Cut					⌘X
Copy					⌘C
Paste					⌘V
Duplicate					⌘D
Select All					⌘A
Select Labeled					⌥⌘L
Select Unlabeled					⌥⇧⌘L
Invert Selection					⇧⌘I
Deselect All					⇧⌘A
Find...					⌘F
Search Adobe Stock Photos...					
Apply Camera Raw Settings					▶
Rotate 180°					
Rotate 90° Clockwise					⌘]
Rotate 90° Counterclockwise					⌘[
Creative Suite Color Settings...					⇧⌘K

Let's say that you want to select 15 out of 20 documents in the Bridge. It's probably faster to press Command-A (PC: Control-A) and then hold down the Command key (PC: Control key) and click on the five documents that you didn't want.

Another way to do this would be to select the five documents you don't want because it's faster and then choose Invert Selection from the Edit menu to deselect those five and select everything else in the folder.

You can deselect all by choosing Deselect All from the Edit menu.

Renaming Documents

Renaming documents in the Bridge is one of the functions I use the most. I like doing it in the Bridge because I can see the thumbnail and move from image to image and rename each one quickly. Here's the big reason it's so easy: when you click on the filename of a document in the Bridge, it highlights just the name and not the file extension. So you can just type without worrying about remembering to put the file extension back in. What's even better is that you can rename a document, press the Tab key, and it will automatically highlight the filename of the next document. This is great because you can quickly name your documents with specific names that apply to the document.

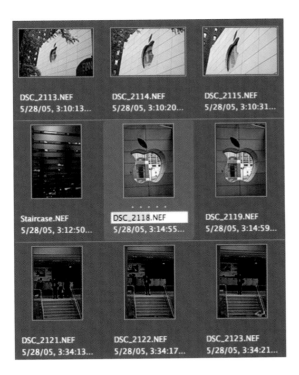

Using Batch Renaming

Renaming the documents individually is great when you want to give specific names to your individual documents. However, if you have hundreds or thousands of documents, you may want to simply give each one a generic name, such as "2005concert," and add a sequence number and file extension. You could thus turn DSC_2120.NEF into 2005concert-01.NEF. The Bridge lets you rename your files in batches. You simply give it the parameters and it will rename all of your selected documents in a flash. This is a very powerful feature called *Batch Renaming*.

Step 1: Navigate to a folder of documents.

Step 2: Select all the documents (Command-A or PC: Control-A) or just the documents you want to rename.

Step 3: Choose Batch Rename from the Tools menu.

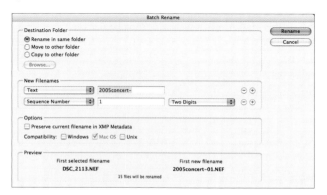

Step 4: When the Batch Rename dialog box appears, you can decide if you want the documents to be renamed in the same folder (in other words, renaming the originals); moved to another folder (so that they are renamed and then physically moved to the folder); or copied to another folder. This last option leaves the original documents untouched and copies and renames the documents to another folder of your choice.

Step 5: You'll probably want to name your documents. From the top pull-down menu, you can change the current filename type to Text and type in your own filename. I put a "-" after my filename so that there would be something to separate it from the sequence number.

Step 6: All of the documents can't have the same exact name. You'll need to add either a sequence number or letter (using the second pull-down menu) that will automatically increment so that each document will have a unique name. You can add this unique identifier by clicking the plus sign to the right of Text, then use the Sequence Number pull-down menu and text box to make your selection.

Step 7: Verify that the naming convention is what you want by looking at the sample at the bottom of the Batch Rename dialog box. If you're happy with your choices, click the Rename button in the upper-right corner of the dialog box.

Rotating Images

Often we take digital pictures or scan images at a 90° angle. Many newer digital cameras have settings to automatically import photos into the computer so they are the right orientation. However, many digital cameras don't offer this feature. You can correct the orientation in the Bridge with a single click. Select the image or images that need to be rotated and click the Rotate 90° counterclockwise button or the Rotate 90° clockwise button at the top of the Bridge window. You can also quickly rotate an image 180° by selecting the image, bringing up the contextual menu, and choosing Rotate 180°.

Although the Bridge allows you to quickly and easily rotate images, the rotation doesn't really happen until you open the file in a graphics application, such as Photoshop or Illustrator, and save it in its rotated state. So if you rotated an image in the Bridge and then dragged it into InDesign, it would appear with its original orientation.

Deleting Documents

There are going to be times when you're looking at images or other documents in the Bridge and you're going to decide that a document is not good enough to keep. It may be out of focus or just too embarrassing. You're in luck. You can delete files directly from the Bridge. If you want to get rid of a document, simply select it and click the trash icon on top of the Bridge window. The selected documents will immediately be removed from your Bridge window. For your safety, the Bridge will simply move the document(s) to the Trash in the Finder (PC: Recycle Bin). So if you trashed something by accident, you can get it back by going to your operating system's trashcan and taking it back out. When you empty the Trash in the operating system, the documents you deleted from the Bridge will then be deleted permanently.

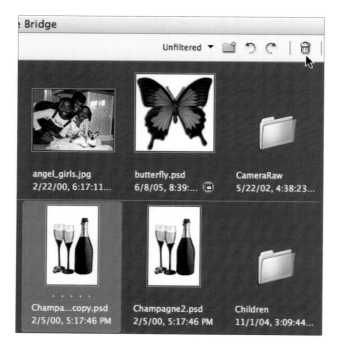

Moving Documents

You can move documents around in the Bridge window from one folder to another using drag and drop. The biggest problem you might have with this technique is that the folder you want to move the documents to may not be open or in view. The Bridge is a one-window application—however, you can have more than one Bridge window open at a time.

Step 1: Choose New Window from the File menu.

Step 2: Navigate to the folder into which you want to move the documents.

Step 3: Go back to the original window and drag the documents from the original window into the folder of the new window.

Or:

Step 1: Add the folder that you want to move the documents to to the Favorites palette.

Step 2: Navigate to the folder containing the documents you want to move.

Step 3: Drag the documents to the icon of the folder you want to move them to in the Favorites palette.

Launching Documents

If you want to open a document from the Bridge into the appropriate application all you have to do (in most cases) is double-click the document. The Bridge will open the document you double-clicked in the default application for that file type. You can see and change the file type associations (for example, .jpg, .gif, .tif, etc.) in the Bridge Preferences.

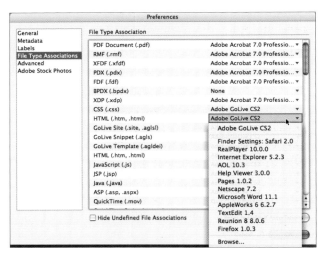

However, rather than change the file type associations permanently, you may want to open a .JPG file this one time in Adobe Illustrator CS2 to trace it, instead of using its default application, Photoshop CS2. You can do this by selecting the document and then choosing Open With

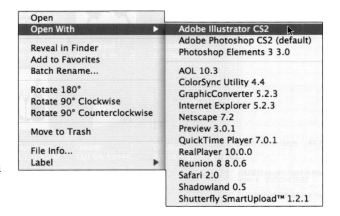

from the File menu. A list of applications that can handle that type of file will be displayed and you can pick the one you want to use to open the file. This will not alter your preferences for the default applications that open these types of files.

If you want to open multiple documents at the same time from the Bridge, select them and then press the Return key.

Revealing Files

Although the Bridge may feel like an image cataloging program from time to time, the Bridge doesn't really import any files. It merely browses the files in the folders you point it to. Therefore, the files really exist in the folders being managed by the operating system. You may need to locate the actual file itself. You can do this by selecting the file or files and choosing Reveal in Finder (PC: Reveal in Explorer) from the File menu. This takes you to the Finder (PC: Explorer) and opens the folder containing the file.

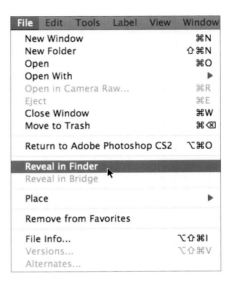

Drag and Drop Folders to the Bridge

Although twirling down the folder tree in the Folders palette allows you to navigate to any folder on your system, it can seem tedious if you have folders nested several levels deep. There is a faster way to get to a specific folder, especially if you were already looking at that folder in the Finder (PC: Explorer). You can drag the folder directly to the Preview area in the Preview palette and the Bridge will automatically start showing you the

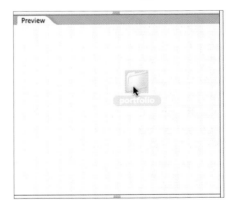

contents of that folder. You could also do this with a CD or DVD. On a Mac, you can also drag the folder to the Bridge application icon either in the Dock or in the Applications folder and it will launch the Bridge, if it's not already open, and show you the contents of that folder.

Entering Metadata

All of your documents will contain some metadata. For example, images contain information from the device that captured them or created them. The Adobe Bridge allows you to enter your own metadata, too. Prior to the Bridge and the File Browser, this was a very laborious task. You used to have to open the images one by one in Photoshop and enter the information in the File Info dialog box and then save the file. Doing a few dozen images could take hours. Luckily those days are long behind us. Now you can select multiple files in the Bridge and enter the metadata all at once in just seconds.

What's the advantage of entering metadata?

The biggest advantage is that it makes your files searchable. For example, if your image is named DSC2004.jpg, you wouldn't know what it was until you looked at it, nor would you be able to search for it unless you knew the name. However, if the file had a description, you could search for text that appears in the description and find it. The Bridge has a Find function that we will discuss later. The metadata actually travels with the file and is therefore searchable by other applications. Mac OS X 10.4 Tiger includes a new search function called Spotlight. Spotlight now searches metadata and the metadata you enter in the Bridge would allow your documents to show up in Spotlight search results.

Step 1: Select one or more documents in the Bridge.

Step 2: Choose the Metadata Focus Workspace from the Window > Workspace menu. This is not required, but it makes the Metadata palette larger and the main focus of the side panel.

Step 3: Scroll down to the IPTC Core field and enter your creator information.

Step 4: Once you've entered all the information about your file, click the Apply button in the bottom-right corner of the Metadata palette. The Apply button looks like a checkmark.

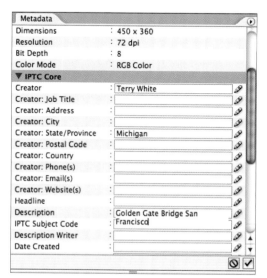

Creating Keywords

In addition to metadata you have the ability to assign keywords to your documents. I look at keywords as categories to group like documents. The Bridge comes with several default keywords, like Birthday, Graduation, and places like New York and San Francisco. Most likely only a couple of these default keywords will apply to you. Therefore, it's important to know how to create your own keywords. It's very easy to do.

Step 1: Bring up the Keywords palette on the left panel.

Step 2: Click the New Keyword button at the bottom of the palette. It looks like a pad of paper.

Step 3: Name your keyword. For this example, I named mine Anniversary.

Step 4: press the Return or Enter key to lock in your name.

You can rename your keywords by Control-clicking (PC: Right-clicking) on them and choosing Rename from the contextual menu.

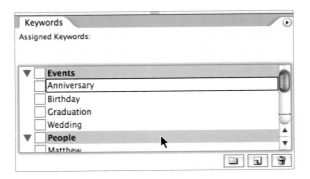

Creating Keyword Sets

In addition to creating keywords, you can create Keyword sets. A Keyword set is the main category for the keywords. For example, you get the default Keyword set Events. Inside Events you'll find keywords like Birthday, Graduation, and Wedding.

To create your own Keyword set:

Step 1: Bring up the Keywords palette on the left panel.

Step 2: Click the New Keyword Set button on the bottom of the palette. It looks like a folder.

Step 3: Name your Keyword set.

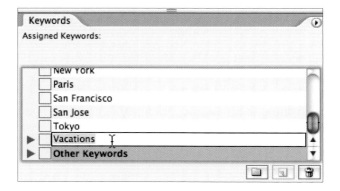

Step 4: Press Return or Enter to lock in your name.

You can rename your Keyword Sets by Control-clicking (PC: Right-clicking) on them and choosing Rename from the contextual menu. Once you have created your Keyword Set you can simply drag and drop your keywords into the sets you've created.

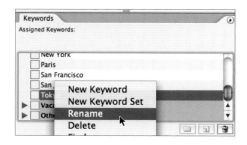
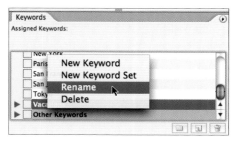

Assigning Keywords

To apply your keywords to your documents, select the documents you want to apply keywords to in the Bridge and then click the checkbox to the left of the keyword that you want to assign. You can assign multiple keywords to your document. For example, you might have an image of the Empire State Building that you took while you were on vacation. You could assign the New York and East Coast Vacation keywords.

Note: Not all file types support embedding this type of XMP data (keywords).

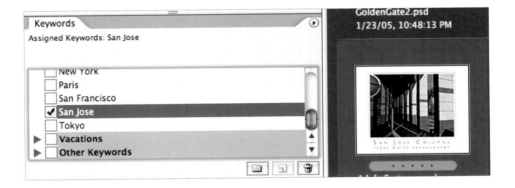

Finding Files

Now that you've assigned keywords to your documents and entered metadata, you can search for your documents in the Bridge. The Bridge offers a powerful Find feature that allows you to search any folder or folders you want.

Step 1: Bring up the Find dialog box by choosing Find from the Edit menu.

Step 2: Choose the main folder you want to search, keeping in mind that you can include the subfolders that it contains.

Step 3: Now choose your Criteria. By default, it wants to look for the filename and if you know what the filename is, you're all set. If not, then you can select the menu that displays "Filename" and choose any of several choices of criteria to search on, such as Keywords or All Metadata.

Step 4: You can search on multiple criteria by clicking the plus sign to add criteria. For example, maybe you want to find your Egypt pictures created before July 21, 1990.

Step 5: You can choose whether or not the search must include all of your criteria or any of it. If you choose *Any*, it would find any documents with the keyword Egypt and any documents created before July 21, 1990.

Step 6: Lastly you can choose to have your find results display in a new browser window.

Step 7: Click the Find button to start the search.

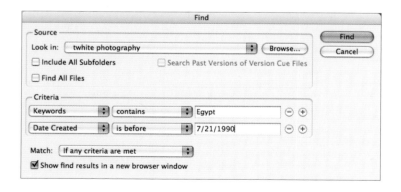

Copying and Pasting Files

I've covered the various ways to move files from one folder to another in the Bridge, however, there are times where you may want to copy a file from one location to another. You can use the drag-and-drop method as you would to move a file: the only difference is that you would hold down the Option key (PC: Alt key) as you move the file and it would copy it instead of moving it to the destination. However, this still requires that you have a view of both the file you are copying and the destination folder. It's easier to simply choose Copy from the Edit menu and then navigate to the folder that you want the copy to be in and Paste the file in that location. You can also do this with multiple files selected.

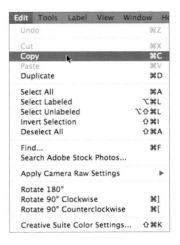

Because there is always more than one way to do something in Adobe products, I feel the responsibility to let you know at least one more way to do this. The Bridge also has a "Duplicate" feature. If you select a file and choose Duplicate from the Edit menu, you will get a new copy of the file in the same location with the word "copy" in the filename. You can then move that copy of the file to another folder and then change the name to remove the word "copy." Although this is another way to do the same thing, I think you'll find the Copy and Paste method the easiest because it feels more natural.

Paging through PDF Files

The Bridge can view PDF files. No big surprise there. If you click on a folder that contains PDFs, the Bridge will automatically start building thumbnails showing you the first page of each PDF. However, what you may not notice right off the bat is that when you click on a PDF file in the main window of the Bridge, it will show in the Preview palette (as you would expect), *and* you'll be able to page through the entire PDF by clicking the navigation arrows at the bottom of the Preview palette. You can also type in a page number in the box to the right of the page navigation arrows and press Return to jump directly to that page. If you use the techniques we've discussed earlier

you'll know that you can expand the Preview palette to make it larger and in effect see all that you need to see in the PDF without opening it in the Adobe Reader or Acrobat. If you double-click on the PDF in the Preview palette, it will open the PDF in your default PDF reader.

Viewing Adobe Illustrator Color Swatches

The Adobe Bridge can view Photoshop, Illustrator, InDesign, and PDF files. However, this is by no means a complete list. These are the kinds of files that you would expect the Bridge to be able to preview. The Bridge can also view several other formats, such as TIFF, JPG, EPS, and QuickTime. The Bridge can view file types that you may not be thinking about, and one of those is the Adobe Illustrator Color Swatch format. This allows you to see the color swatches in the file without having to load the file first in Adobe Illustrator. So even though the Bridge shows you document files that you will open in your applications, it will also show you files that can be used in your applications that aren't necessarily documents.

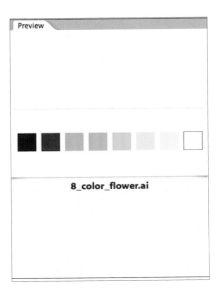

Viewing Non-Adobe Files in the Bridge

Hard as it might be to believe, it's not just an Adobe world. This means that from time to time you may have documents that were not created in Adobe products. These documents show up in the main Bridge window when you click on a folder. Unfortunately, not all documents will show a preview on the icon of what the document contains. However, that doesn't mean that you can't use the document. If you browse a folder in the Bridge that contains a Microsoft Word document or a FileMaker database file, for example, you won't see the contents of these files, but you can double-click on the file to open it and it will open it in the appropriate application. So if you double-click on a Microsoft Excel document it will open in Microsoft Excel. Keep in mind, though, that if you drag and drop a non-Adobe file into an Adobe application window that supports it, the file you dropped will be placed in the document. So if you open an InDesign CS2 document and create a frame, you can drag a Microsoft Word document from the Bridge window into the InDesign CS2 frame and it will place the Microsoft Word document onto the page into the frame.

Using Contextual Menus

I can't stress the importance of contextual menus enough. The Bridge has contextual menu support throughout the application. Keyboard shortcuts are great, but they require that you commit them to memory. When you invoke a contextual menu it allows you to see the options that are most commonly used for the document or the part of the application that you clicked on. On the Mac you invoke a contextual menu by either holding down the Control key and clicking the mouse, or, if you have a mouse with two or more buttons, you can usually use the right button on the mouse to bring up the contextual menu. On the PC you would use the right mouse button. Depending on the document or folder that you click on, the Bridge will offer a contextual menu of the options that you can perform with that document type.

 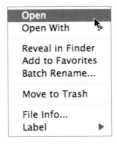

4 Bridge Scripts

Adobe Bridge comes with scripts that allow you to run operations on the files that you select in the main Bridge window with the other CS2 applications you have installed. If you only have a single product from the Creative Suite 2 (other than Photoshop CS2), then you may not have any Bridge scripts, as the Creative Suite or Photoshop CS2 installer installs them. The Bridge scripts appear under the Tools menu next to the name of each application. What's cool is that from time to time Adobe and third-party developers may offer additional Bridge scripts for you to download. As of the writing of this book, there are already some pretty cool new scripts released that you can download: http://share.studio.adobe.com/adBrowseSubmit.asp?c+222.

Photoshop Scripts for the Bridge

Photoshop CS2 offers the most scripts for the Bridge. This is due largely to the fact that most of these functions existed in the Photoshop File Browser before the Bridge came onto the scene. So it was a natural fit for Adobe to move these functions over to the Bridge. Let's take a look.

The Photoshop Batch Script

The Batch script is the first Photoshop script in the Tools > Photoshop menu. When you select one or more images in the Bridge window and choose Batch from the Tools > Photoshop menu, you'll be able to run predefined Photoshop actions on the images you selected. The script will launch Photoshop CS2 and immediately bring up the Batch dialog box and reference the images from the Bridge. You can then choose which action you want to run from the popup list and run the action on your selected images.

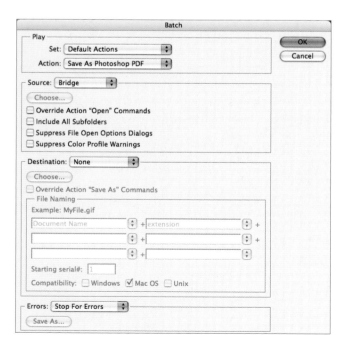

The Photoshop Contact Sheet Script

Contact Sheets are made up of multiple thumbnails of single-page Photoshop documents. For example, if you were going to burn your images to a CD or DVD and you wanted to have a visual record of what you burned on the disc, you could use the Contact Sheet script to build that Contact Sheet for you in the Bridge. To use this script, select one or more images (you probably want at least two, otherwise you could simply print the single image). Then choose Contact Sheet II from the Tools > Photoshop menu. Photoshop CS2 will launch or come to the foreground and present you with a dialog box to set up how you want your Contact Sheet to look.

If you are going to make an insert for your CD/DVD jewel case then you probably want to change your dimensions to 4"x 4"and change the number of rows and columns to four each. When you click OK, Photoshop will build a new document for your new contact sheet. If you have more than 16 images selected, Photoshop will continue building new documents until it runs out of images. You can then print each page out, trim them, and insert them in your jewel cases.

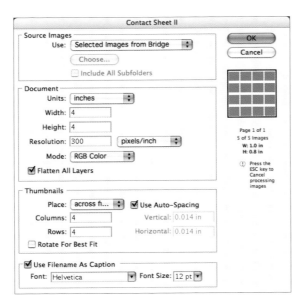

The Photoshop Image Processor Script

If you regularly work in Photoshop, chances are you're doing the same operations over and over again. The Image Processor script covers a couple of functions that I do almost daily. For example, I convert images to JPEG or TIFF and I need them to fit a certain pixel dimension. You could create your own custom action to do this in Photoshop, but then you'd have to change the action every time one or more of the parameters changed. The work has been done for you with the Image Processor script. Select the images you want to process and choose Image Processor from the Tools > Photoshop menu. In the Image Processor dialog box, you can decide if you want the images to be processed to the same location or to a different folder. You can pick the file type you want and even choose multiple file types in case you need a JPEG for emailing and PSD for working with the highest quality image you can get. Optionally, you can choose to resize the images to fit a certain pixel width or height (it's probably best to pick one or the other as picking both could lead to a distorted image if the aspect ratio is not the same). Lastly, you can choose to run an additional action and embed your copyright info or ICC color profile. You can save your settings to an external file and load them back in as needed so that you don't have to remember them from session to session. Once you've made your selections, click Run to begin the processing in Photoshop.

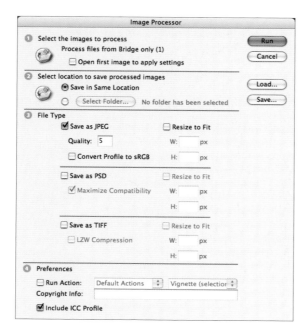

The Photoshop Merge to HDR Script

Photoshop CS2 introduced the HDR (High Dynamic Range) function. High-end and prosumer photographers will use the HDR command to combine multiple images of the same scene to capture the dynamic range of the scene into a single HDR image. So if you shot the same exact scene using different settings on your camera to bring out the highlights in one shot, the shadows in another shot, and the midtones in another shot you could merge them together using the HDR command to produce a single image that would be nearly impossible to capture in one shot. The images must all be the same size and should be shot with a tripod and be the same exact scene. If you have two or more images that meet this criteria, you can select them in the Bridge and choose Merge to HDR from the Tools > Photoshop menu. Photoshop CS2 will start merging the images and then present you with a dialog box so that you can preview the result.

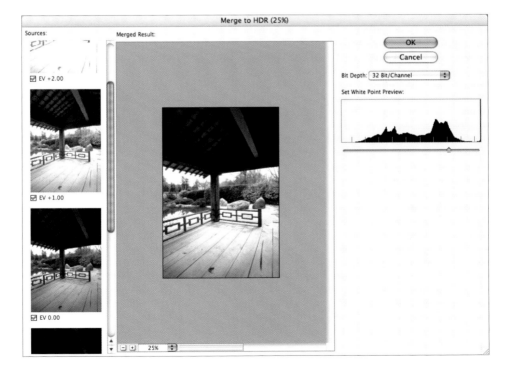

The Photoshop PDF Presentation Script

The PDF Presentation function allows you to easily share your images with people who may not have a photo-editing tool or you can use it to send someone a Group of images via email. The next time you want to either create a multiple-page PDF of your images or a presentation that goes full screen and advances automatically, select your images in the Bridge and choose PDF Presentation from the Tools > Photoshop menu. Photoshop will launch or come to the foreground and bring up the PDF Presentation dialog box. You can then choose between a simple Multi-Page Document or a Presentation that plays automatically on the recipient's computer. If you do choose Presentation, you can then set it to advance automatically by the number of seconds that you want, choose whether it will loop or not after the last page, and set whether or not you want transitions between the slides. Once you make your choices, click Save and you will be given the opportunity to pick the destination folder and filename as well as set your PDF options for compatibility, compression, and security.

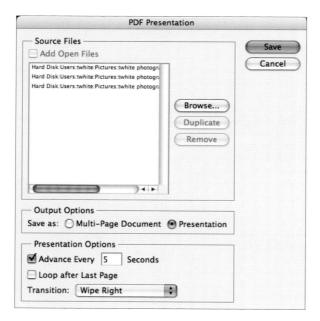

The Photoshop Photomerge Script

Photomerge has long been a favorite of mine as it allows you to shoot a panoramic scene as multiple shots and then join those shots together afterwards in Photoshop. You can also use Photomerge to combine images together that were scanned in multiple pieces because your scanner couldn't accommodate the large format of your print. When you have images to combine, select them in the Bridge and choose Photomerge from the Tools > Photoshop menu. Photoshop CS2 will launch or come to the foreground and automatically start opening your images and looking for overlap so that it can align them into one panoramic or merged scene. Once it's done, it will show you a preview from which you can apply additional settings, such as Advance Blending and Perspective. When you click OK in the dialog box, Photoshop CS2 will build your merged photo and create a new document in Photoshop.

The Photoshop Picture Package Script

Picture Package will make you a hero among friends and family. It allows you to take your photographic masterpiece and create a sheet of photos at various sizes so that you can print one sheet of photos and not waste paper. You start by selecting at least one image in the Bridge and then choose Picture Package from the Tools > Photoshop menu. Photoshop CS2 will launch or come to the foreground and then present you with the Picture Package dialog box. Your selected image will be there in the default layout; you can choose your Page Size, Layout, and Resolution. There are other options, such as Label, which will print below each picture, but in most cases you're not going to want labels taking up the space. Once you have your settings, click OK.

There is a secret tip for the Picture Package. Let's say that you want the majority of the pictures on the page to be of one person or one shot, but you want to selectively swap out one or more of the images for different images. You can do this by simply clicking on the image you want to swap out while it's in the Layout preview in the Picture Package dialog box. The Select an Image dialog box will appear allowing you to choose a different image for that spot.

The Photoshop Web Photo Gallery Script

Occasionally you'll want to show your images on the Web. After all, it's the "in" thing to do. Most ISPs offer Web storage space as part of the monthly agreement, which means that you can upload your own HTML pages to your Web space via FTP or WebDAV. Adobe offers a great HTML authoring tool with the Creative Suite 2 Premium called GoLive. However, you have an easier tool for this task. You can use the Web Photo Gallery script without having to know anything about creating HTML.

To get started, select the images that you want to post on the Web as a gallery. Choose Web Photo Gallery from the Tools > Photoshop menu and Photoshop CS2 will launch or come to the foreground. Next, Photoshop will present you with the Web Photo Gallery dialog box asking you to pick a style for your gallery. There are several to choose from, and the new Photoshop CS2 even includes some Macromedia Flash-based ones. Although you have the option to enter your email address, it's not required and you probably shouldn't use it unless you really need to, otherwise you could be inundated by spammers. You can then choose a Destination folder for your gallery to

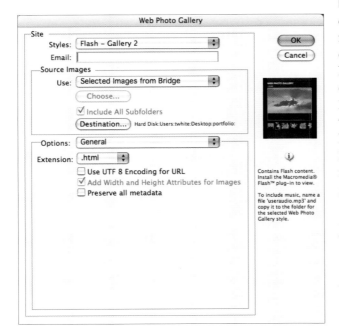

be built in and choose options for your thumbnail/image sizes and captions. Once you have your settings set, click the OK button and Photoshop will go to work building your gallery. Once it's complete, Photoshop will automatically launch the gallery index.html page and show it in your default Web browser. You can then use an FTP utility to upload the page to your hosted Web space.

Illustrator

At the time this book went to press there were only a couple of Illustrator Bridge scripts. By the time you read this, there could be several new ones available to download from the Adobe Exchange site.

The Illustrator Live Trace Script

Illustrator CS2 has the ability to automatically trace bitmapped images and create beautiful vector artwork from them. The process involves creating a new document, placing the bitmapped graphic on the page, selecting it, and clicking the Live Trace button on the Options bar. However, if you have several images to trace and you want to do it in batches, you can do so from the Bridge with the Live Trace script. Select one or more bitmapped images in the Bridge. Choose Live Trace from the Tools > Illustrator menu. In the Live Trace dialog box in the Bridge you can pick your settings. You can choose a preset for your trace settings. You can choose to vectorize all the documents to individual layers in a single document or leave this option unchecked and Illustrator will generate a new document for each bitmapped document you have selected. You can then choose a destination folder for your new files and even pick a naming convention for the new files. If you don't use a new naming convention, the script will use the original document name with the .ai file extension. Click OK to let the script run.

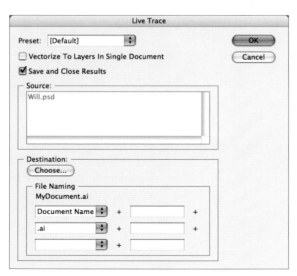

The Illustrator Export to Flash Script

If you have a multiple-layer Illustrator file, you can convert that file to an ani-
mated Flash (.SWF) file that could be put up on your Web site. There are two
ways to go about this—one way doesn't give you any control and the other
does. There are two scripts in the Export to Flash menu. One is called Quick
Export and the other is called Custom Export. Choosing Quick Export gives
you a straight export to .SWF format with no options. This would be useful
if you just wanted to put a vector logo up on the Web and have it remain as
a scalable vector in the Flash format. However, if you want to control your
export options and enable the layers to SWF frames options, you're going
to want to choose the Custom Export from the Tools > Illustrator menu. The
Export to Flash dialog box appears, and here you can control how your layers will be treated in the .SWF file as well as the appearance, animation, and
image quality. Once you have the settings set the way you want, click OK to
generate your .SWF file.

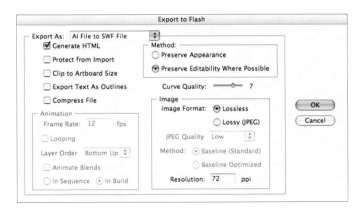

InDesign

At the time this book went to press there was only one InDesign Bridge script. Although there's only one, it's a very cool one that allows you to make a contact sheet in InDesign. By the time you read this, there could be several new ones available to download from the Adobe Exchange site.

The Create InDesign Contact Sheet Script

We've already covered creating Contact Sheets in Photoshop. So you may be wondering, "why is there a need for InDesign to be able to create Contact Sheets, too?" There's one answer to that, and it's "flexibility!" With a Photoshop contact sheet your data will all be converted to pixels at a single resolution. So even if you included vector images, they would be converted to bitmaps on your contact sheet. InDesign is resolution independent. Therefore, you can include both raster and vector images on your InDesign

contact sheet pages and they will print at whatever resolution your printer supports. Also it's a lot easier to swap out images in InDesign frames than it is from Photoshop layers.

Select your images in the Bridge and choose Create InDesign Contact Sheet from the Tools > InDesign menu. The Contact Sheet dialog box appears, which allows you to specify the settings for your Contact Sheet pages. You can choose how your images will be placed, either Across First or Down First. You can then choose how many columns and rows you want. Next you can choose your spacing options for how close the images will be to each other and whether or not you want the images to rotate to fit better. As with the Photoshop contact sheet, you have the option to include a caption under each picture. What's really cool is that you can use an InDesign template to customize the look and feel of your Contact Sheet pages. This really broadens the possibility for this script as it could be used for things like yearbooks, scrapbooks, or photo albums. You also have the option to output directly to PDF. Once you're happy with your settings click OK and watch it work.

Script Manager

Now that we've taken a good look at the scripts that come with the Creative Suite, I want to remind you that third parties can also create scripts. If you know JavaScript, you can even create your own scripts. Once you start getting additional scripts you'll probably want some way to control which ones load and which ones don't. The Bridge gives you this control with the Adobe Script Manager. You can open the Script Manager by choosing it from the Bridge menu (PC: Edit menu). You'll be able to click on each script and get a full description of what the script does and choose whether or not the script should load on startup of the Bridge. At the bottom of the window you'll be able to see the path to where your scripts are located. Also by default the Bridge is set to automatically load new scripts. You can disable this check box if you want.

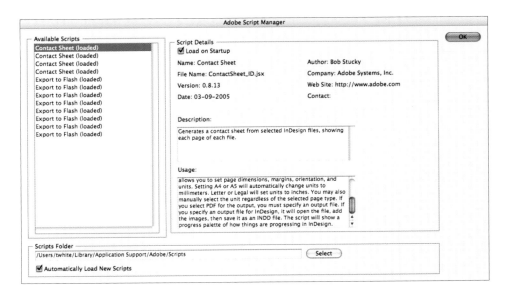

5 Adobe Stock Photos

When Adobe introduced the Creative Suite 2 they also introduced the new Adobe Stock Photos service. Many of you use stock photos today and many of you don't. For those of you that do, you'll find it pretty addicting that you can search for stock photos, download unwatermarked comps, and use them immediately in your layout without ever launching a Web browser. Adobe has done a seamless job of integrating this new service directly into the Creative Suite 2 applications and the Bridge. Before we get to how it works, let's first cover some of the common questions:

Royalty Free or Rights Managed?

These images are royalty free, which means once you purchase them you can use them for life. That comes at a price, of course. Royalty-free images tend to cost more because you only have to buy the image once and you can use it forever.

Are these Adobe's images?

No! These are the same images that you would buy directly from the stock photography houses. As of the writing of this book, the Adobe Stock Photos service uses images from Photodisc by Getty Images, Comstock Images, Digitalvision, Imageshop, and Amana. However, instead of having to go to each of these providers separately, you can do your searches in the Bridge and it will search all five image houses at once. Since this service is Web based, Adobe can add new providers at any time.

How do I buy an image?

Images are purchased via credit card right in the Bridge. The Bridge includes a shopping cart feature that allows you to add images to it at any time and check out whenever you're ready. You'll be able to see the prices for the various sizes as well as any restrictions, if any.

Now that I've answered the most common questions up front, let's get started on how this works!

Searching for Images

Searching for images by keyword is a natural. If you're looking for images of Caribbean cruises, then you're likely to put "Caribbean cruise" in the search field and press Return. That's exactly how the Adobe Stock Photos works.

Step 1: Click on Adobe Stock Photos in the Favorites palette.

Step 2: Click into the Search field and type in your keywords. You can either click the search button (the binoculars) or press Return on your keyboard.

Step 3: The Bridge will start searching all of the stock photography houses for your keywords and display images that match your keywords. Near the top of the window you will see how many hits you got. You may only be seeing the first 50 of the total results. If you don't find the image you want there, you can click More Results to see the next 50.

Getting Prices and Keywords

Now that you've found some images that match your keywords, you may be curious as to what the image costs or you may want to find similar images that are based on keywords that you may not have included in your search. The Adobe Stock Photos service allows you to get all the keywords that apply to a particular image as well as the prices at the various resolutions. All you have to do is click on the image you want this info for and then click the Get Price & Keywords button located at the top of the Bridge window. This opens a new window showing you the prices at the different resolutions that this image is available at, as well as the keywords associated with this image. You can then check off which keywords you want to use in an additional search to find similar images and click the Search Again button to perform the next search.

Downloading Comps

Probably the coolest feature of the Adobe Stock Photos service is that you can download unwatermarked low-resolution comp images and use them in your mockups. When you find stock images that might look right in your layouts or you're not quite sure which one your client will want to go with, you can simply click the Download Comp button near the top of the Bridge window and your selected image(s) will be downloaded to your hard drive to the Downloaded Comps folder (which you can see in the left panel). Once a comp has been downloaded, you can double-click it to open it in Photoshop or simply drag it from the Downloaded Comps folder directly into your InDesign or Illustrator layouts. You don't have to worry about remembering which image house holds the image; if you ever want to know that information you just select the comp and look at the Metadata palette. It will show you the keywords associated with that image as well as the provider, if you scroll all the way to the bottom.

Purchasing Images

As of the writing of this book, the only way to purchase an Adobe Stock Photo image is through the Bridge via your credit card. Existing accounts and purchase orders that you have with the providers aren't accepted here. The process for purchasing an image is pretty straightforward. You simply click on the image to select it, and

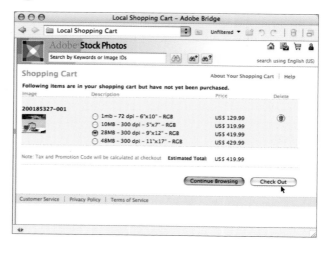

then click the Add to Cart button at the top right of the Bridge window. The Bridge gives you a message stating that the image has been added to your cart and a button allowing you to view your cart. Next you'll either have to sign in with your existing account or create a new account (if this is your

first purchase). Like most online shopping experiences, this is a secure transaction and you have to agree to the royalty-free license agreement. Then you can click the Purchase button to begin your download.

I should mention that this kind of download should only be attempted on a high-speed Internet connection, as you are downloading images that are quite large. Once the image(s) has downloaded it will be located on your hard drive in your Purchased Images folder in the left panel. You can keep the images there or you can move them to any folder you like. They're yours at this point. If for some reason the image doesn't download completely or properly, you can always check the Download Status window by clicking the Open Download Status button at the top of the Purchased Images window or by choosing it from the Window menu. This will show you any downloads in progress or any downloads that didn't complete.

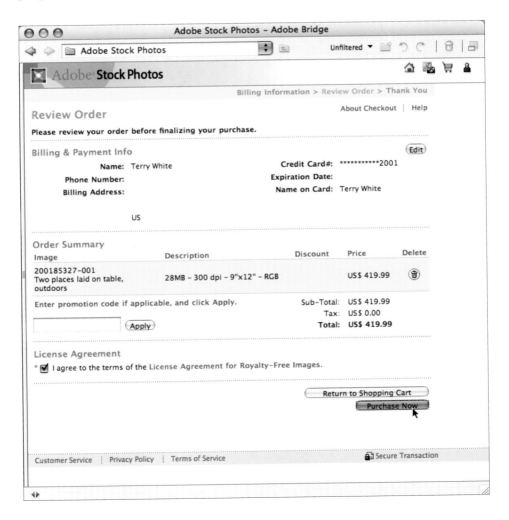

Viewing Previous Searches

Okay, so you did a search last week and you want to do the same search again today. You're in luck. The Bridge keeps track of all your previous searches. All you have to do is click on the Previous Searches folder in the Favorites palette and you'll see each search that you've performed represented as a folder with the date and time that the search was performed. The folder will be titled with the keyword(s) that you used for the search. Now all you have to do is double-click on the folder you want and it will show you the results that you got the last time. At this point you can then click the buttons to Get Price & Keywords, Download Comp, or Add to Cart.

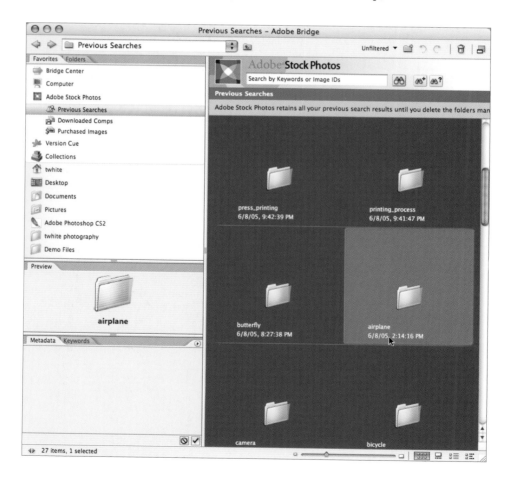

Finding the Right Stock Images

Let's face it. Searching through stock photos doesn't always yield the exact image you want. With this in mind, Adobe has added a Photographers Directory Search button to the Bridge. This button takes you to the Web and allows you to search for professional photographers in your area who can shoot that perfect image for you.

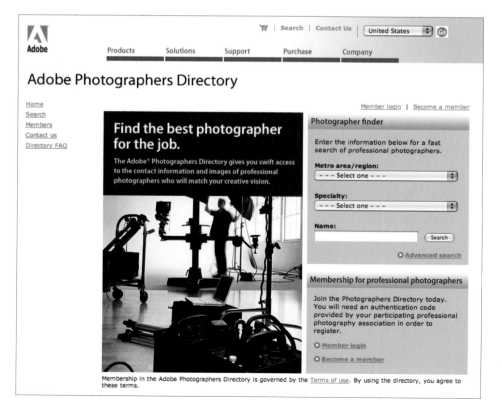

6 Integration

Although the Bridge offers all kinds of built-in capabilities, it is also tightly integrated with the other Creative Suite 2 applications. InDesign CS2 takes unique advantage of the Bridge by using it as a template browser and allowing you to see the colors and fonts used in a particular document or template without having to open it. In the case of Photoshop there are several new printing services that can be accessed directly in the Bridge. This will allow you to order prints, photo books, calendars, and other items using your images. Adobe Acrobat PDFs can be previewed page-by-page in the Bridge without having to open them first in Acrobat.

Previewing InDesign Document Fonts & Colors

You have probably already discovered or read earlier in this book that the Bridge will preview InDesign CS2 documents as thumbnails. What you may not have noticed right away (because it's a secret!) is that when you click on an InDesign document and look at the Metadata palette, it will show you the fonts that are used in the document as well as the defined color swatches.

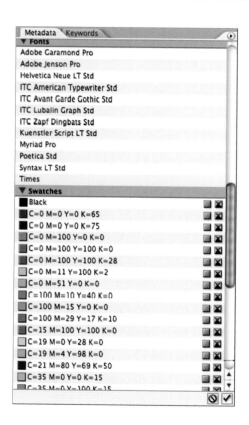

Working with InDesign CS2 Templates

InDesign CS2 comes with dozens of professionally designed templates. There is a really easy way to get to them from InDesign's welcome screen. If you've already closed the welcome screen or chosen not to show it at start up, you can get to it again by choosing Welcome Screen from the InDesign CS2 Help menu. From the welcome screen, choose New from Template.

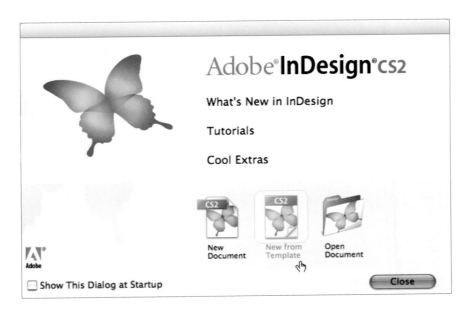

This takes you to the Bridge and to the special location of the InDesign CS2 Templates. The templates are saved as Collections. You can access the category of templates that you want by either double-clicking on the Collection or by double-clicking on the corresponding folder. If you double-click on the Collection, it will open it in a new Bridge window. If you double-click on the folder, it will open in the same Bridge window.

Now that you see the templates, you can also browse them in the Preview palette. Just click on a template that you're interested in and the Preview palette will show you the cover page. You can also click through the pages by using the left and right on screen arrow buttons.

Using InDesign CS2 Snippets

InDesign CS2 allows you to save portions of a layout as a "snippet." You can select the elements on your page and drag the selection to the desktop or to a specific folder. That's great! What's even better is that you can drag these snippets to any open folder in the Bridge and you will get a thumbnail that represents the components of the snippets. You can then drag them from the Bridge to any open InDesign document page.

For you page layout gurus out there, this may sound very familiar. It sounds like the "Library" function that page layout applications have had for years. You're right, it does sound like the Library feature. However, snippets are far more flexible. A Library is a separate document that has to be opened inside InDesign to access the Library contents. However, snippets remain independent elements that can exist in any folder. If a Library becomes corrupted, then you have to build it over again from scratch or use your last back up. If one snippet becomes corrupted it doesn't affect the other snippets.

Using Photoshop Services

Adobe Photoshop Services are integrated into the Bridge. These services allow you to order high-quality prints that can be sent directly to you or your customer and are provided through Adobe and Kodak. From the Bridge, you can order prints, photo books, calendars, and greeting cards. You can also use the Photo Sharing feature to send your friends, colleagues, and clients online photo albums from which they can order prints, photo books, etc. It's great having these services integrated into the Bridge. It means that it's just one less reason to work outside the Bridge and since you've already organized your images and rated them, it's a natural.

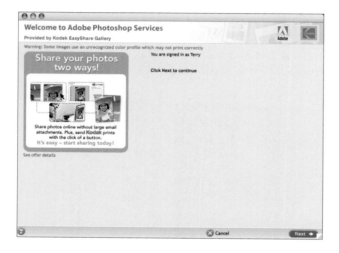

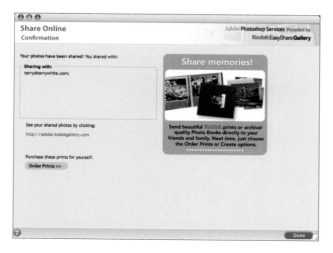

Launching the Bridge from Other CS2 Applications

In Adobe Photoshop 7 and CS you could access the File Browser by either choosing Browse from the File menu or by clicking the Browse button on the Options bar. In Photoshop CS2, you can use these same exact methods, however, it will launch the Bridge, or if the Bridge is already running, it will bring it to the foreground. That's great if you're in Photoshop, but what if you're in Adobe InDesign CS2, Illustrator CS2, or GoLive CS2? You're in luck! It works the same way in those apps, too. There is a Browse menu item under the File menu as well as a "Go to Bridge" button on the Options bar in each one of those apps. So you can get the Bridge easily and quickly no matter which CS2 application you're in.

Using the Place Command

Although the CS2 applications support drag and drop from the Bridge into your open documents, the whole window management thing can be a pain. I like to keep my Bridge window and my document window open at the full size of the screen. So, to drag an image from the Bridge into InDesign, it means either going into Compact Mode or physically moving the Bridge window over so that I can see my InDesign document in the background. Luckily there is another way to do this. It's called the "Place" command. The way it works is that you create or open a document in one of the CS2 applications, such as InDesign. Although you can use this command for Photoshop, Illustrator, InDesign, or GoLive you will probably use it the most working with InDesign, as InDesign is the application that you'll constantly be placing documents into. In many cases this will be a better workflow (using the Place command from the Bridge as opposed to using the Place command in InDesign and then having to go locate the images you want to bring in) for some InDesign users because you will be able to find your images in the Bridge using the Find command or Favorites, select the one or ones that you want to place, and then choose Place In InDesign from the File menu. The Bridge will toggle you over to InDesign by bringing InDesign to the foreground and giving you the Place icon. You can then click on your page where you want the image to be placed and InDesign will create a frame on the fly and place the image in the frame. If you create a frame first in InDesign, you can select it, return to the Bridge, and then select your image that you want placed. Next choose Place In InDesign from the File menu in the Bridge and when InDesign comes to the foreground the image you placed will be in the selected frame.

Finally, if you select two or more images in the Bridge and choose Place In InDesign, the Bridge will place all of the selected images on the current page in InDesign in their own individual frames. The images will likely overlap and need to be repositioned. When you have two or more images selected in the Bridge and use the Place In InDesign command, the Bridge will ignore any selected frames in the InDesign document.06-08.tif.

7

The Bridge Center for the Creative Suite Only

Although the Bridge ships with any of the stand-alone CS2 applications, it also ships with the Creative Suite 2 Standard and Premium Editions. When you get the Bridge as part of the Creative Suite 2 you get a few more features. One of those value-add features is the Bridge Center. The Bridge Center is like having a default page in a Web browser. Many people have default Web sites such as my.yahoo. The default page for the Bridge with the Creative Suite 2 is the Bridge Center. The Bridge Center provides you with easy access to your most recently accessed files and folders as well as any saved collections. The Bridge Center also offers access to the synchronized color management capabilities across the CS2 applications, the CS2 Help System, and the ability to create new Version Cue projects. In addition to these useful features, there is also a built-in RSS (Really Simple Syndication) reader and a Tips and Tricks section. Although these are wonderful things to have at your fingertips, use of the Bridge Center is totally optional. Also, in order to use the RSS reader, you will (of course) need a connection to the Internet.

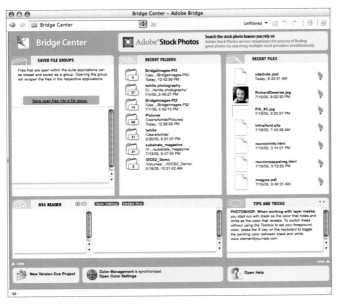

Using the Bridge Center for RSS Feeds

In this day of information overload and having just about any piece of information at your fingertips, it almost becomes impossible to stay up on everything you're interested in. That's why most news sites now offer RSS (Really Simple Syndication) feeds. An RSS feed typically consists of a headline and one or two lines of the article. This way you can quickly skim the headlines from your favorite sites and then, if something piques your interest, you can click on it to find out more details or read the full article. So it's like having news as it happens at your fingertips. The old-fashioned way would be to have your favorite sites load across your Web browser and then you would need to look at them constantly and refresh them throughout the day to see if anything changed. That's the way I used to surf the Web. Now I almost completely rely upon RSS feeds. It's much easier, and I don't feel like I'm shackled to my computer as much.

To use the Bridge Center's RSS reader you must first go find an RSS feed to subscribe to. To find an RSS feed, you'll need to use your Web browser. Go to a news site such as cnn.com. Most news sites will either display a button/link called RSS or XML. In the case of cnn.com, you'll see a link at the bottom of the page called "Add RSS Headlines." The site may also refer to the RSS feed as simply, "feeds." Once you find the RSS or XML button on the site you're interested in subscribing to, clicking on it will likely bring up a page of gibberish in your Web browser. That's because RSS feeds are XML based and most Web browsers don't know what to do with this code directly. So instead of clicking on the button, Control-click (PC: right-click) on it and choose Copy URL from the contextual menu. Then return to the Bridge and click the add (+) button to bring up a dialog box where you can paste in the URL to your RSS feed. Then click OK, and the Bridge will go out and return with headlines from the RSS feed that you typed in.

Working with Collections in the Bridge Center

When you search in the Bridge using the Find command you may realize that you want to perform that search on a regular basis. The Bridge allows you to save your search criteria as a collection. To do

this, choose Find from the Edit menu or press Command-F (PC: Control-F) on the keyboard. Once your results have been displayed, you can then click the Save As Collection button in the upper-right corner of the Bridge window. You'll get a dialog box that allows you to name your new collection. You'll also notice that there is no option to choose where to save the collection. That's because the Bridge automatically puts all collections in the same place. If you look in the Favorites palette you'll see the collections icon. Once you click on the Collections item in the Favorites palette the Bridge shows you a window of all your saved collections. Now if you double-click on any of your saved collections the Bridge will perform the same search and show the results with all the files that match, even if the files were added after the collection was created.

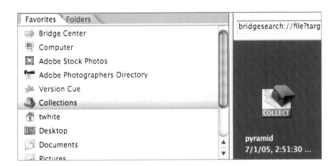

Creating Saved File Groups

Creative projects often involve documents created in multiple applications. For example, if you were working on a brochure and you were creating the logo in Illustrator, retouching the photos in Photoshop, and doing the layout in InDesign, you probably want to have those documents available to you at a click of the mouse. You're in luck because there is a feature that does that very thing in the Bridge Center. It's called Saved File Groups. I also refer to this feature as the "End of the Day" button. That's because at the end of the day you probably have several documents open and you need to close them all and then open them all again in the morning. The Save Open Files Into a Group command does exactly that. In this example, I had two Photoshop documents and one Illustrator document open. I clicked the Save Open Files Into a Group command located on the Bridge Center window. A dialog box appeared that asked me to name the Saved File Group and then I clicked OK. The two Photoshop documents and the Illustrator document were then closed and the Saved File Group was created. Now whenever I want to open those same documents again I simply click on the Family Vacations Saved File Group and an area under the heading Saved File Groups will open up that shows me the number of Photoshop documents and Illustrator documents that it contains. When I click anywhere in that section all three documents will open in their respective applications.

Using Synchronized Color Management

Many of the users that I talk to simply don't get what "Synchronized Color Management" means. So let me try to explain it. Synchronized color management in the Bridge lets you make all your color management settings the same across your Creative Suite applications. Many users start out getting Photoshop calibrated to the exact color settings they need to produce good quality photographic prints. Or maybe you're a layout person and you need to be assured that what you see in InDesign is as close as possible to what will be produced on press. The beauty of "Synchronized Color Management" is that it doesn't matter which application you start with. Once you set up the color management settings in one of the Creative Suite applications, all you

have to do is save those settings and give them a name in the app of your choice. Next, go to the Bridge Center and click the Open Color Settings button at the bottom of the screen. You will see a dialog box with the default color settings as well as the settings that you created in the CS2 app. Choose the one that you created and then click the Apply button. Now at the bottom of the Bridge Center window it should say, "Color Management is synchronized." This means that all of your CS2 apps will now have the same color management settings and colors should look consistent across your CS2 applications.

Creating Version Cue Projects

Version Cue is the file management and versioning feature of the Creative Suite. We touched on it a little in Chapter 1. With Version Cue you can set up projects and manage versions of documents within those projects. Version Cue is not really a stand-alone application. It's actually server technology that works in the background to assist you in managing versions of your CS2 documents. The Bridge allows you to create new Version Cue projects and see the documents within them just as you would any other folder. The big difference is that instead of saving multiple versions of a document and having to come up with your own naming scheme, Version Cue manages the versions for you. For example, say you were creating a logo in Illustrator and working with a client on various revisions that they requested. You could open the logo each time there was a change to be made, make the change, and click Save. However, every time you hit Save, you have completely over written the last version of the logo. If your client then comes back to you and says, "You know, I changed my mind. I really liked the one from two days ago better," you would then have to scramble to put the logo back to that state. This is easier said than done in most cases.

Before Version Cue, to avoid overwriting your documents, you had to save each change as a new document and come up with some kind of naming convention such as ABClogo-01.ai and then ABClogo02.ai and then ABClogoFinal.ai and then, of course, there would be another change and now you have to go with ABClogoFinal2.ai or ABClogoReallyFinal-I-Mean-It-This-Time.ai. Version Cue eliminates this dance by keeping track of the versions for you. It also allows you to include comments with each version that you save and it allows you to promote a previous version to be the current version of a document.

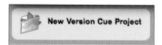 Although each of the CS2 applications allows you to create Version Cue projects, it's easier to do this when you're in the Bridge Center. Simply click the New Version Cue Project button at the bottom of the Bridge Center window.

You'll get a dialog box asking you to name your project and allowing you to include details about your project (optional). You can also allow others to access your Version Cue project by clicking the "Share this project with others" check box. Once you click OK, the project will be created and the Bridge will open an empty window, which is actually the folder for your Version Cue project. The window will be empty because you haven't saved any documents into it yet. Now when you're in one of the CS2 applications with an open document and choose Save As, as long as you use the Adobe dialog box—which is a feature you can toggle by clicking the Adobe Dialog button in the lower-left corner of the Save As dialog box of any CS2 app—you'll be able to choose the Version Cue Project that you want to save into as well as giving it the initial comment. From that point on when you want to make further revisions you choose Save A Version from the File menu of your CS2 app and you'll be presented with a dialog box that lets you put in comments about that particular version. You won't have to give it a file name again or choose a location. Version Cue will manage these tasks for you.

8 Working with Camera Raw

Camera Raw was the final piece that fell into place to make digital photography truly professional. Most mid-range to high-end digital cameras being sold today shoot in Raw format. What that means is that the camera saves the highest quality uncompressed image that it can directly to your memory card. All digital cameras being sold today shoot in JPEG format by default. However, with JPEG there is some image quality lost almost immediately after snapping the picture. This is due to the JPEG format itself, which is a lossy format that throws away some information to make the file smaller. You usually lose some color and some definition in the image—the higher the JPEG compression, the more you'll lose.

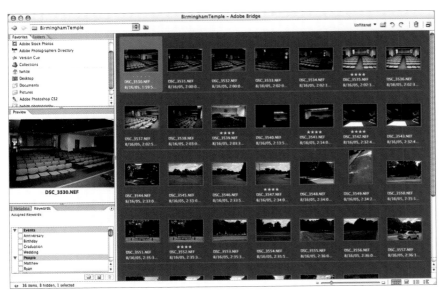

Camera Raw, on the other hand, doesn't compress the picture or throw any information away at all. More and more professional photographers are shooting in Camera Raw format exclusively for this reason. If your digital camera supports shooting in Raw format, you would simply choose that setting on the camera. One problem with Camera Raw, however, is that each camera manufacturer has its own Raw format, and usually these cameras come with their own proprietary software for processing the images. But there is good news. Don't even bother taking the CDs out of the box that your camera came in. If you have the Adobe Bridge you can do your Camera Raw image processing in a familiar environment. All you have to do is download your images from your camera into a folder on your hard drive. Once they're in a folder you can then navigate to that folder using the Bridge and the Bridge will start building thumbnails for each of the Raw images.

Applying Camera Settings

Double clicking on a Camera Raw file will usually launch Photoshop, and
Photoshop will present you with the Camera Raw dialog box. This allows
you to do some initial corrections to the image, such as adjusting its expo-
sure and temperature. But this kind of work can be time consuming when
you have more than a few Raw images to go through. Once again, enter the
Bridge. It allows you to select multiple Raw files at once and then bring them
all up in the Camera Raw dialog box so that you can apply the same settings
to multiple files or simply toggle through them, applying individual corrections to the images that need them. Once you select your Raw images in the
Bridge, choose Open in Camera Raw from the File menu or press Command-R
(PC: Control-R). This brings up all of your selected Raw files in the Camera
Raw dialog box.

You can then Shift-click on each image that you want to make the same adjustments to. This is handy when you're adjusting images that were shot in the same light. You can also use the Crop, Straightening, and Rotation tools at the top of the Camera Raw dialog box on multiple images at the same time. Simply click on the next image you want to adjust and continue making adjustments to all the Raw images that need adjusting. Once you've made your adjustments you can then click the Done button and your settings will be applied. If you want those images to always be adjusted with the same settings each time you make an adjustment, you can click the Synchronize button in the top left of the Camera Raw dialog box. This is extremely cool for making adjustments down the road and it even allows you to adjust the crop of all of the synchronized images at the same time. The Raw files will not be altered. Instead, the Bridge applies the settings so that when the Raw files are opened in Photoshop or batch processed into other formats those settings will apply then. If you wanted to make further adjustments using Photoshop CS2, you can then simply click the Open button to open the selected images in Photoshop.

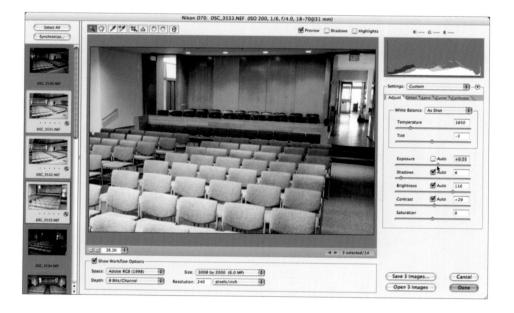

Using Camera Raw Batch Processing

Prior to the Bridge you would typically open each image one by one and go through the Camera Raw dialog box so that the image could then be opened in Photoshop and saved in a format (such as JPG, TIFF, or PSD) that could be used in other applications. With the Bridge, you have Camera Raw batch-processing abilities. Let's say that you shot 100 Camera Raw images and they are sitting in a folder on your hard drive. Now you want to create 100 JPEG files from those Raw files so that you can show them to your client via email. Or perhaps you need 100 PSD files so that you can place them in your InDesign catalog. Simply select the 100 images in the Bridge and choose Open in Camera Raw from the File menu or press Command-R (PC: Control-R) on the keyboard. When the Camera Raw dialog box appears you can select your 100 images by clicking the Select All button in the upper-left corner of the window. Then click the Save Images button in the lower-right corner of the dialog box.

You'll get another dialog box that allows you to pick your format and naming options as well as choose a folder for the resulting files.

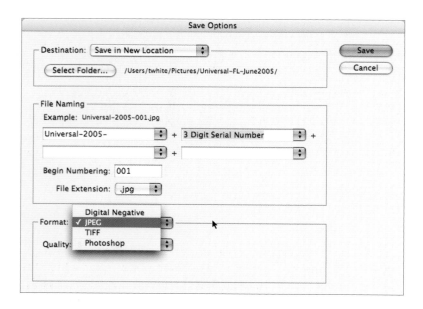

When you click Save, the Bridge begins processing these images in the background. You won't have to keep the Camera Raw dialog box open. You can click the Cancel button in the Camera Raw dialog box and go back to the Bridge and continue working. This will not cancel the background processing of your images. However, if you do cancel the Camera Raw dialog box you won't have any other indicator to let you know when your processing is complete. While the Camera Raw dialog box is open there will be a status line just above the Save button that tells you how many images remain to be processed.

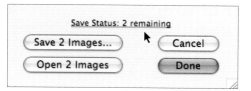

9
Cache Management

The real power behind the previews in the Bridge is the Cache. The Bridge builds cache files each time you navigate to a folder of files from which the Bridge can build thumbnails. This means that the next time you access that folder the thumbnails and metadata will appear much faster. By default, the Bridge builds one large centralized cache file on your hard drive. There is an option in the Bridge preferences to change this setting to "Use Distributed Cache Files When Possible." The graphics experts are on both sides of the fence on this topic. Some believe that one large cache file is better, while others believe that having a separate cache file for each folder is better. I guess it really boils down to the way you work. If your folders move around a lot

especially from drive to drive, then you're probably going to want to go with distributed cache files that stay with your folders. Also keep in mind that even if you go with a distributed cache, the Bridge will still need to build a centralized cache to cache those folders that can't be written to. For example, if you navigate to a CD-ROM with images on it the Bridge will build a cache for the contents of the CD-ROM but it will do so on your hard drive.

Building a Cache for Subfolders

When you navigate to a folder that contains subfolders, the Bridge only builds a cache for the main (parent) folder. It won't build a cache for the subfolders until you actually *open* the subfolders. You can tell the Bridge to do this process in the background ahead of time by choosing Build Cache for Subfolders from the Tools > Cache menu. The Bridge will automatically build a cache for all the subfolders in the main folder and in the background.

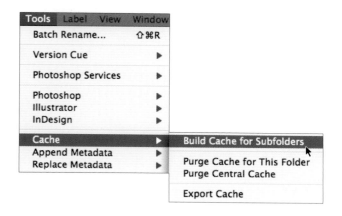

Purging the Cache

If you navigate to a folder and feel that the thumbnails are outdated or aren't all there, you can choose "Purge Cache for This Folder" from the Tools > Cache menu. Keep in mind that when you purge the cache for a folder or the centralized cache you will loose ratings and labels that you have applied to files that can not have metadata written directly to them.

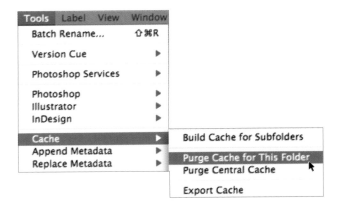

Exporting the Cache

At some point you will probably want to burn your images/documents to a CD or DVD. This is a common procedure when you're archiving projects that you have completed. It would be great if when you put the CD/DVD back in your computer at some point in the future and browsed it with the Bridge, the Bridge didn't have to build a cache again. You can make your wish come true by exporting the cache. When you choose Export Cache from the Tools > Cache menu, the Bridge builds a cache and places it in the folder that you're currently viewing.

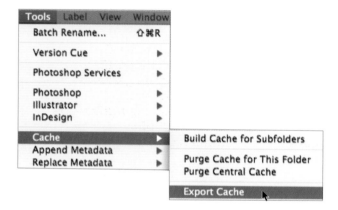

These files are invisible and therefore it will feel like nothing happened when you run this command. However, you can verify that they are truly there by choosing Show Hidden Files from the View menu. Now when you burn this folder or move it to another location it will have the cache file in it. The next time you view this folder with the Bridge, even after it's burned to a disc, the Bridge won't have to build the thumbnails.

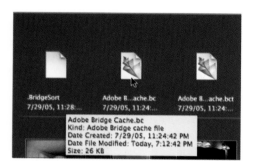

Index